The Black Sheep B
Cookbook Volume 1

The companion workbook and notes to our Video Cookbook Volume 1

Contents

©2011 Rick & Diana Boufford and Just Good Fun
www.justgoodfun.net and www.blacksheepcookingclub.com

EAN-13 # 978-1456340186   ISBN-10: 1456340182

Just Good Fun P.O. Box 15427, Newport Beach, CA 92659-5427

Introduction

I feel fortunate to not only have survived but to have succeeded for almost thirty five years in the restaurant and hospitality industry. Twenty two of those years where spent as the working chef and sommelier at The Black Sheep Bistro in Tustin, California, along with my wife and partner, Diana. This experience, combined with our many culinary adventures to Europe, has given me a unique perspective on food & wine and the sharing and teaching of it to others.

That said, know that this is not a traditional cookbook, it's a workbook. It's a tool to take into the kitchen and work with, get dirty, write on, and in. It was written for 2 levels of cooks; some will know what to do just from the book alone but many, especially those with less experience, will want to use it alongside the DVD this book is taken from, **"The Black Sheep Bistro's Video Cookbook Vol 1."** There, the same dishes were taped "looking over my shoulder." I'm convinced this standing next to me style presents the best how to cook learning format because you see the whole process exactly the way it was done in The Black Sheep kitchen during the shift. The dishes are real, nothing is left out, and there are no magic tricks.

I'm pleased to add this workbook to the Black Sheep Cooking Club's mentoring tool chest. It's both the entire menu I got to serve at The Black Sheep Bistro but more than that, it's the culmination of some of my favorite dishes I have had the good pleasure to work with and create over the years in the business. Many are originals, and some are, The Black Sheep Bistro's version of ...

Now, let's learn to cook, and make these dishes your own!

Rick Boufford
Chef
The Black Sheep Cooking Club

To begin - A Chef's Salt or Seasoning Mix

This is the rock bottom ingredient in many professional kitchens. It's what defines the very essence of the restaurant and gives each and every dish it's unique characteristic. Apprentices around the world know that if you take a particular restaurant's Chef Salt or Seasoning recipe with you and use it in another restaurant, you're not only a thief, you may well be banned from working in any kitchen, anywhere. Many of the top restaurants guard these kinds of season mix recipes with great care. In some restaurants, only the chef or owner knows the exact recipe and makes all of it, him (or her) self. Here's a couple of mine;

Rick's Chef Salt

4 parts white salt
I part granulated onion
I part ground black pepper
I part ground celery
1/2 part white pepper
I part Spanish paprika
I 1/2 parts granulated garlic

Play with this and make it your own!
More/less garlic, white pepper, onion or?
Make different versions using Cumin for a Middle East feel,
Cayenne Pepper for a spicy version. There's so much more!

These recipes are in parts so you can use anything; spoons, cups, hands whatever depending on how much you want to make at a time. Another advantage to a seasoning mix above is, you cut the salt (or sodium) in the dish drastically.

Many are amazed at the difference just these two ingredients can make on whatever it is your presenting. Both raw and cooked foods can benefit and will seem to come alive in brand new ways.

Rick's Herbs de Provence

4 parts whole dried Thyme
2 parts whole sweet Basil
2 parts Summer Savory
I part Fennel Seed
I part Lavender Flowers
(Extra additions - Chervil, Parsley, Marjoram)

Try making the recipes as written first. Then experiment and make them your own!

Fun foods from France & Spain

Featuring the full flavored Catalon inspired dishes from France & Spain.

Appetizers

Sauces for sides or dipping; Aioli, La Rouille, Basil, Tarragon, or Cilantro. *- in "Extras"*

Fresh Goat Cheese - with crispy garlic toasts. *- page 6*

Tri Shrimp - With Aioli, spicy la Rouille & Cilantro Aioli. *- page 6*

Escargot - In the shells with garlic butter *- page 7*

Cantimpalitos - The little Spanish sausages with garlic mashed potatoes. *- page 7*

Spanish Sausage Plate - An assortment for 2. *- page 8*

Iberian Pen-Style Dates - Sweet dates stuffed with Sobrasada, wrapped in jamon. *- page 8*

Tomato Salad- Marinated baby grape tomatoes & aged Sheep's milk cheese. *- page 9*

Mussels Salchichon - With 2 kinds of sausage, onion, garlic, and potatoes. *- page 9*

Mussels Catalana - Steamed with potatoes & Aioli or spicy La Rouille. *- page 10*

Mussels Provencale - With garlic, parsley, and olive oil. *- page 10*

Papas Bravas - Potatoes served with a spicy cayenne pepper sauce. *- page 11*

Mushrooms Jerez - With garlic, herbs, & Sherry. *- page 11*

Baby Lamb Chops (3) With garlic and herbs. *- page 12*

Grilled Quail - With garlic and herbs. *- page 12*

Salads
- Salads in the "Main Course" section

Small - Large

Choice of;

| Classic French style mixed baby greens with tomatoes and croutons | Black Sheep Caesar style made with Romaine and served with Sheep's Milk Romano & croutons. |

Dinner Salads

You can add;
4 Shrimp - Today's Fish - Boneless Lamb Loin
Duck Breast - Quail 1 bird or 2 birds - Confit of Duck
New York Steak - New Zealand Baby Lamb Chops

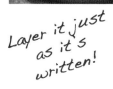

Layer it just as it's written!

The Black Sheep Bistro's
Fresh Goat Cheese Appetizer
Fresh Goat Cheese "Pyramid"
Fresh Basil
Julienne Sun Dried Tomatoes
Herbs de Provence & Rick's Chef Salt
Sprinkle with Olive Oil & Balsamic Vinegar
serve with Fresh Baked Garlic Crouton Slices

People asked, "Why does your shrimp taste so good?"

Tri-Shrimp Appetizer
Large (u15 or larger) top quality
Mexican #1 white Shrimp
(3 pieces per plate)
1 spoon each Aioli Sauce,
Cilantro Aioli Sauce, and La Rouille Sauce
(see videos for each)
Grill Shrimp and serve with each of the sauces.

We used "Wild" Mexican #1 White Shrimp!

Make the butter, stuff the snails in the shells and bake in a hot 450° oven 'till bubbling!

Escargot in Garlic Butter

(for details see Garlic Butter in extras section)
Blend - 1/2 cup each whole garlic cloves, diced onion and loosely chopped fresh parsley with 1/4 cup extra virgin olive oil. Then add - 1/2 # butter
1/2 tsp Ground Black Pepper
1/4 tsp Ground White Pepper
1 (+) tsp Rick's Chef Salt
This butter should be well seasoned!

Cantimpalitos from La Espanola...

...Grilled (keep 'em moving)

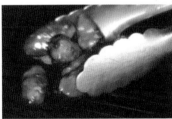

Served on Garlic Mashed Potatoes!

The Black Sheep Bistro's Cantimpalito Appetizer
Simply grill 3 to 6 Cantimpalito Sausages per person and serve on a bed of Fresh Garlic Mashed Potatoes

The Black Sheep Bistro's
Spanish Sausage Plate
Simply grill Cantimpalito & Butifarrita Sausages
Add slices of Jamon Serrano & Cantimpalo
Serve with a bed of
Fresh Garlic Mashed Potatoes – *Recipe in " Extras" section!*

We used La Española's sausages!

Cut & stuff dates, bake and serve on a small green salad.

The Black Sheep Bistro's
Iberian-Pen Style Dates
Thin Sliced Spanish Ham
Sobrasada Sausage
Pitted Dates
bake in a hot 450° oven 4 to 6 minutes
and serve with a small amount of Salad Mix,
sprinkled with Olive Oil, Spanish Vinegar
Rick's Chef Salt & Herbs de Provence

I love this vinegar!

The quality of the vinegar, olive oil...

...and the sweetness of the grape tomatoes makes it!

Tomato Salad
In a bowl combine;
Minced Garlic, Herbs de Provence, Salt,
Rick's Chef Salt, Balsamic Vinegar, Olive Oil
and Fresh Chopped Basil.
Cut the Sweet Grape Tomatoes in halves,
mix well, plate, and top with
Fresh Sheep's Milk Romano Cheese!

Mussels, potatoes and sausages, a great combination!

Mussels Bilbao
Fresh, live, small black mussels, bearded
(8 to 15 pieces per person, see Cleaning Mussels video)
Potato, Onion, Chorizo Bilbao & Butiffarita
all cut into a 1/4 inch dice
Rick's Chef Salt
1 tsp each Dried Parsley & Italian Herbs
1 Tbsp + Minced Garlic & 1/2 cup + Water
Steam, Season and Serve!

The Black Sheep Bistro's
Mussels Catalana

Fresh, live, small black mussels, bearded
(8 to 15 pieces per person, see Cleaning Mussels video)
Steam Mussels and Potato cut into a 1/4 inch
dice in 1/2 cup + Water
Thicken with Aioli Sauce
(or La Rouille Sauce if you want it spicy,
see Aioli or La Rouille video)
Season with Rick's Chef Salt and serve!

Hard to beat the simple combination of potatoes and aioli!

Here the seasoning of the mussel sauce makes the dish! (Also, you can use white wine instead of water.)

Mussels Provencale

Fresh, live, small black mussels, bearded
(8 to 15 pieces per person, see Cleaning Mussels video)
Extra Virgin Olive Oil
Rick's Chef Salt
2 tsp Dried Parsley
1 Tbsp + Minced Garlic & 1/2 cup + Water
Steam, Season and Serve!

Simple - Fried potatoes with a spicy garlic sauce!

The Black Sheep Bistro's
Papas Bravas
Diced Potatoes
Approx 1 to 2 Tbsp Canola Oil
La Rouille Sauce
1/2 tsp water
Rick's Chef Salt
Fresh Parsley
Saute potatoes until brown, drain and sauce!

This also makes a great sauce for lamb, chicken or a great steak!

The Black Sheep Bistro's
Mushrooms Jerez
Olive Oil, Unsalted Butter, Minced Garlic,
1 tsp each Parsley & Italian Herbs,
Quartered Cremini Mushrooms
Sweet Cream Sherry
Water (if needed)
Rick's Chef Salt & Salt (if desired)

11

Baby Lamb Chops

Smear Fresh Baby Lamb Chops with;
Minced Garlic, Herbs de Provence,
Rick's Chef Salt & Olive Oil.
Grill; turn sideways, then over,
then sideways again!
Serve with Garlic Mashed Potatoes,
and Olive Oil, Herbs de Provence
and Rick's Chef Salt to dip into.

Lamb Chop Tips – Don't overcook!
Always try to use fresh not frozen!
(Frozen will be dryer!)

Quail was on the menu
because I love it!
We used
Manchester Farms.
(Don't overcook them!)

Grilled Quail Appetizer

Smear fresh Quail with;
Minced Garlic, Herbs de Provence,
Rick's Chef Salt & Olive Oil.
Grill; turn sideways, then over,
then sideways again!
Serve over rice, with Olive Oil, Herbs de Provence
and Rick's Chef Salt to dip into.

Notes!

Notes!

Main Courses

Dinner Salads - *pages 14 & 15*

Baby New Zealand Rack - Baked with 2 kinds of mustard and Herbs de Provence. - *page 16*

Spicy Lamb Harissa - 3 large California Lamb Chops with a spicy cayenne pepper/garlic sauce. - *page 17*

Baby New Zealand Lamb Chops Dragoncello - 6 chops with a Tuscan Tarragon/Garlic sauce. - *page 18*

Boneless Loin of Lamb "Catalana" rolled in cracked black pepper, grilled and served with Aioli. - *page 19*

Lamb Chops Spanish Style - 3 Large chops baked with garlic, olive oil & herbs. - *page 20*

Matt's Surf-n-Turf - We grill 3 baby lamb chops & 3 shrimp and serve them with Aioli. - *page 21*

Duck Breast "Steaks" - Grilled skin off, with a Honey Lavender sauce. - *page 22*

Pato Mio (My Duck) - A grilled Duck Breast with Lavender and a leg of crispy confit. - *page 23*

New York Steak - With Spanish style mushrooms & Sherry. - *page 24*

The Spanish Grill - 2 baby lamb chops, semi-boneless quail and 2 kinds of sausage. - *page 25*

Quail Provençal - 2 semi-boneless grilled with olive oil, garlic and Herbs de Provence. - *page 26*

Shrimp a la "French/Mex" - Two cultures reunite with this spicy Cilantro Aioli. - *page 27*

Seafood Sobrasada - Shrimp, today's fish, mussels, sausages, potatoes and vegetables. - *page 28*

Today's Fresh Fish with Aioli, La Rouille, Cilantro or 1/2 & 1/2. - *page 29*

Chicken Breast - A boneless double breast, choose; Aioli, La Rouille, Tarragon, Harissa, or Cilantro.
\ *page 30*

Paella & Fideos

Paella - Spanish Rice Dishes - *page 31*

*Paella "Oveja Negra" - Seafood & veggies w/black "Valencia" rice. (min. 2)

*Paella "Parellada" - Saffron "Valencia" rice with lamb, chicken, shrimp, sausages, mussels and vegetables. (min. 2)

Fideus - Catalan Pasta Dishes - *pages 32 & 33*

Choose; saffron, "blanco" (no saffron), or rojo (tomato) base.

Seafood Fideo - With shrimp, mussels, fish and vegetables.

Mixed Fideo - With shrimp, mussels, chicken, sausages & vegetables.

Veggie Fideo - Mixed vegetables.

Fideo Rustico - The lamb, sausage, onions, garlic, and mushrooms make it's own base.

We offered two basic salads;
Baby Greens and an "eggless Ceasar".
You could then choose to have
whatever you wanted on top.

Our grilled shrimp and
grilled Wild Salmon salads
were both very popular.

People didn't believe us when we told them it was the same dressing for both salads.
But the dressing on the Romaine and the added Sheep's Milk Romano Cheese,
made it taste very similar to a Ceasar Salad.

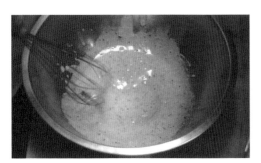

Duck Breast Salad

A typical "Mesclun" mix of Baby Greens.

Black Sheep Salads

The printed dressing recipe is in the "Extras" section!

See the video in the Extra's section to make
Rick's House Dressing,
then let your imagination take over!

We made our salads with everything we had! Shrimp, fish, lamb, New York Steak, just vegetables or something cheesy. But our most requested was our Duck Confit Salad.!

Baby Lamb Racks

(These were extremely popular!)

Bake with;
1/2 Mustard 1/2 Whole Grain Mustard Sauce
and Herbs de Provence

*Try this simple mustard blend
on other things also!*

Serve with Garlic Mashed Potatoes
(or Baked Potatoes) & vegetables!

*Smear the rack with a generous amount
of the mustard sauce, sprinkle with
Herbs de Provence, then bake at a
high heat (450° to 500°) for 12 to 15 minutes.*

At home it might look like this!

Smear some great quality
lamb chops with Harissa Sauce...

Spicy Lamb Harissa

See our Harissa video for the sauce recipe.

Simply smear the chops with Harissa and bake. Serve with rice and vegetables of your choice!

Bake in a 450° (+) oven
for 6 or 7 minutes...

And Eh Voila! Quick and wonderfully spicy!

Baby New Zealand Lamb Chops "Dragoncello"

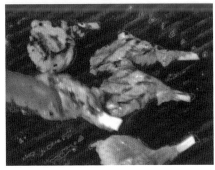

See our Tarragon Aioli video for the recipe, then simply grill the chops to medium rare, and serve with Garlic Mashed Potatoes and vegetables of your choice!

Serving hot food in a restaurant is a timing issue. The plates have to be set and ready so as soon as the meat is done it's plated and sent out hot off the grill! Below the Tarragon Sauce, potatoes, vegetables and garnish await the chops.

Lamb Loin Catalana

Simply smear the Lamb Loin with coarse Cracked Black Pepper and grill.

Two lamb lions with cracked black pepper await the grill.

Serve with Aioli (see Aioli Video), Garlic Mashed Potatoes (Video also), and vegetables of your choice!

To make sure we were always serving the best meats possible, I sliced the meats at an angle before plating them. It not only looked good, it allowed me to check the doneness and tenderness before going to the customer!

Spanish Chops

(So simple, so good!)

Simply smear the chops with;
Minced Garlic, Rick's Chef Salt,
Herbs de Provence, drizzle with
Extra Virgin Olive Oil and bake.

(Lots of)
Serve with Aioli (see Aioli Video),
rice and vegetables of your choice!

If there were any oil on the tray, along with the juices from the lamb, made a second sauce that was poured on top.

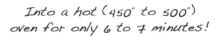

To get the chops so they'd cook more even, I'd use the palm of my hand to press the chops into the same thickness!

Into a hot (450° to 500°) oven for only 6 to 7 minutes!

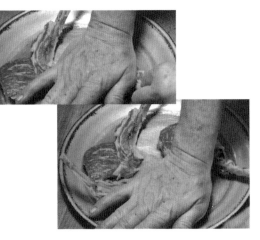

Matt & Delanie's Surf n Turf

**Simply grill 3 Large Shrimp and
3 Seasoned Baby Lamb Chops and
serve with; Aioli (see Aioli Video),
Garlic Mashed Potatoes (Video also),
and vegetables of your choice!**

*This dish was a special request
from two 13 year olds. We ended up
putting it on the menu and it was
extremely popular!*

What could be better? Grilled Shrimp & Lamb...

...on Aioli Sauce!

Duck Breast Steaks

**Simply grill two skinless Duck Breasts
(although for salads I saute with the skin on)
and serve with the sauce of choice.
See our videos for;
Lavender Sauce, Berry Sauce, Aioli,
La Rouille, Tarragon Aioli or Salads!**

Serve with rice and vegetables of your choice!

We sliced the duck breasts before plating.

(My employees will tell
you the special treat
for the night was to
sprinkle the cutting board
with chef's salt and lap
up the duck juices with
bread. So good!)

Pato Mio!

**Simply grill 1 skinless Duck Breast
or pan saute 1 skin-on Breast
and serve with the sauce of choice.
Cook and "crisp" one leg of Confit!**

**Serve with Garlic Mashed Potatoes
(or rice) and vegetables of your choice!**

Refer to video to "steam and crisp" up the duck.

*Crisp up the Confit
Place the cofit skin side up in about
3/4" water, lid and steam 7 to 10 minutes*

*Duck Confit is a detailed process
that involves food safety issues.
Please see Confit in the "Extras" section
and even more details on the video.*

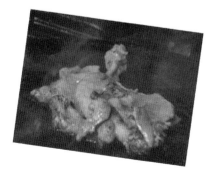

*Now place the Confit on a hot
(I like cast iron) pan skin side
down until brown and crisp.*

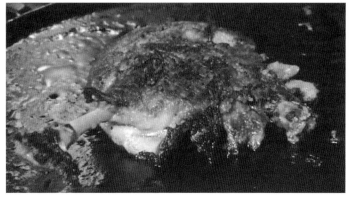

(This picture is skin side up for display only!)

New York Steak
with Mushroom Sherry Sauce

**Grill the New York Steak
Cook sliced Shallot in Unsalted Butter and
Extra Virgin Olive Oil. Season with Parsley,
Italian Herbs and Rick's Chef Salt. Add
Sliced Mushrooms cook till soft then
add (water?) Cream Sherry and
season again!**
Serve with Garlic Mashed Potatoes & vegetables!

Rub on the seasonings before placing the staeks on the grill.

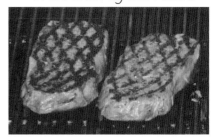

Turn the steaks sideways to give grill marks and keep them from charring too much.

(grill marks image)

What can be better than mushrooms in butter on grilled steaks?

26

The Spanish Grill

(A personal favorite!)

**Simply grill; 1 Seasoned Quail,
2 Seasoned Baby Lamb Chops,
1/2 Chorizo Bilbao & 1/2 Butifarrita
serve with rice and
vegetables of your choice!**

*Season and rub with;
minced garlic,
Rick's Chef Salt,
Herbs de Provence,
& Extra Virgin Olive Oil.*

This is a great "summertime BBQ" dish!

*The sausages
(Bilbao & Butifarrita)
came from La Espanola!*

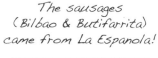

27

Quail Provençal

**Simply grill two Quail seasoned
with Minced Garlic, Rick's Chef Salt,
Herbs de Provence and a drizzle
of Extra Virgin Olive Oil!**

**Serve with Garlic Mashed Potatoes (or rice)
and vegetables of your choice!**

I love the elegant taste of grilled quail. Great on salads too!

Shrimp French-Mex

**This is all about the sauce,
and great quality shrimp!
Make the Cilantro Aioli (see video)
Grill up (4 to 8 per person)
U-15, #1 White, Wild Mexican Shrimp.
Serve with Garlic Mashed Potatoes,
and vegetables.**

*I lovingly called it Frech-Mex
because the Aioli is French and
Cilantro (which the French rarely use)
is a definate Mexican seasoning.*

*Our Cilantro Aioli is a great sauce that was very popular with all kinds of
seafood, chicken and more. But it really stood out with the grilled shrimp!*

Seafood Sobrasada

Gets it's name from the rich Sobrasada sausage from La Espanola.

In a pan heat; Extra Virgin Olive Oil, Onions, Minced Garlic, Chopped Tomatoes, Julienne Red and Green Bell Peppers, torn bits of Sobrasada Sausage, Shrimp, Mussels, Fresh Fish and 1/2" cubed Potatoes. Add Parsley, Italian Herbs, & Rick's Chef Salt then add 1 cup water, lid it, steam/season/plate and serve!

Put all the ingredients in a saute pan, add (hot) water, lid & steam (till potatoes are done, about 7 mintues), remove, plate, garnish and serve!

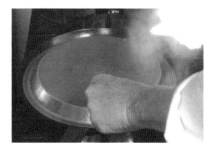

To Bake:

Olive Oil

Minced Garlic

Herbs de Provence

Rick's Chef Salt

Olive Oil

Fresh Fish
(Some of the ways we did it at the Black Sheep!)

Grill and serve with any of our Aioli sauces
or
Bake with Garlic, Rick's Chef Salt, Herbs de Provence & Ex Virgin Olive Oil
or
Or -> **Bake with Harissa Paste**
Serve with Garlic Mashed Potatoes
(or rice) & vegetables!

To Grill;

Start "presentation" side down.

After a couple of minutes turn sideways to give grill marks,

Turn over > and then shortly after turn sideways again.

This helps to keep the fish from charring.
Most fresh fish is best when cooked medium at most!

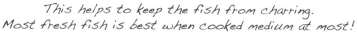

Chicken:

Grilled with Cilantro Aioli

Baked with Harissa!

Chicken
Grill and serve with any of our Aioli sauces
or
Bake with Garlic, Rick's Chef Salt,
Herbs de Provence & Ex Virgin Olive Oil
or
Bake with Harissa Paste
Serve with Garlic Mashed Potatoes
(or rice) & vegetables!

When cooked properly, fresh chicken should be very moist!

I like to season before putting it on the grill.

Like all our meats, remember to turn sideways, turn over when white on edges.

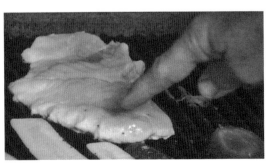

Baked

Grilled

I'd start with the seasonings and vegetables.

Then the meats. When done remove the meats.

Add the water and rice and I choose to continue to stir every once in a while until cooked to the desired doneness. Then add the meats on top and decorate!

I let it set about 15 minutes THEN carefully brown the bottom on low! (About 10 to 20 minutes.)

Paella Parellada

Our "House Paella" with a little of everything.
Assorted vegetables;
Onions, Garlic, Red & Green Bell Peppers,
Tomatoes, Beans and/or Green Peas, Chicken,
Assorted Sausages, Lamb,
Seafood; Shrimp, Fish and Mussels.
The "Valencia Rice" is seasoned and colored
with Saffron, which makes it yellow!

In the restaurant we had to make sure every Paella was perfect, so...

Paella Oveja Negra

This is our "Black Sheep Paella"
made with assorted vegetables;
Onions, Garlic, Red & Green Bell Peppers,
Tomatoes, Beans and/or Green Peas.
Seafood; Shrimp, Fish and Mussels.
The "Valencia Rice" is seasoned and colored
with Cuttlefish Ink to make it black.

I start a Fideo the same way I start a Paella!

Fideo Rustico

Onions, Garlic, Mushrooms with Sobrasada, Bilbao, and Butifarrita Sausages, Fideo (pasta), And Sliced and Grilled Lamb Loin.

Veggie Fideo

Anything you want it to be!

All our Fideo's are seasoned with Salt, Rick's Chef Salt, Parsley and Italian Herbs.

Some of the great things about a Fideo are;
It's fast, you don't pre-cook the pasta.
It's easy, everything is cooked in the same pan.
It's flavorful, the pasta takes on all the flavors!

Have everything cut and chopped and this goes together fast!

Mixed Fideo

**We use; Onions, Garlic, Red & Green Bell Peppers,
Tomatoes, Beans and/or Green Peas (Mushrooms?)
Shrimp, Chicken, Sausages and Mussels.
The "Fideo" can be seasoned and colored
with either Saffron (which makes it yellow),
Tomato Paste (our "Rojo") or left plain (Blanco).**

Seafood Fideo

**Same as above, just use more Shrimp and Mussels, add
Fresh Fish and omit the Mushrooms, Chicken & Sausages.**

*Just like Paella, cook, take out what you don't want
overcooked, add the water, fideo pasta, cook till pasta
is done (about 7 mintues) finish and decorate!*

Notes!

Desserts

Gateau au Chocolat (House Specialty)
The Black Sheep adaptation of the famous chocolate mousse cake from St. Tropez on the French Riviera!

page 36

Crema de Catalonia
Spain's creme brulee!
Rumor (and history) suggest creme brulee is actually a Spanish invention.

page 36

Italian Sundae
(Chef's Favorite)
Vanilla bean ice cream with our dark bittersweet chocolate sauce topped with a hot espresso.

page 37

Profiteroles
(Diana's Favorite)

page 37 *Freshly made cream puffs with vanilla bean ice cream and our own dark chocolate sauce.*

Guido
Another group of favorites combining layered hazelnut and vanilla bean Gelato on a chocolate cookie topped with a dark bittersweet chocolate sauce and hazelnuts!

page 39

Fresh Berries
Your server will inform you of today's selection.

page 38

Black Sheep Tart
Different all the time.

page 39

Chocolate Mousse
We use the finest Belgium bittersweet and milk chocolates for this world renown favorite.

page 38

White Truffle
Passion fruit sorbet, surrounded by white chocolate ice cream, dipped in pure white chocolate, and served with our white chocolate sauce.

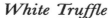

page 39

Dark Chocolate Truffle
Raspberry sorbet encased in chocolate Grand Manier ice cream, dipped in dark chocolate and served with our dark chocolate sauce.

page 39

Lemon Sorbet
Light and refreshing.

- And -

Chef's La Fantasia
A surprise three tiered assortment of fun!

page 39

page 40   (See Dark Chocolate & White Chocolate Sauces on page 41!)

37

Combine water, butter and chocolate, melt over low heat

Combine egg yolks, flour, sugar, vanilla. Add the chocolate mixture.

Whip egg whites (till still moist) fold into mix.

Put into springform pans, bake 375° about 15 minutes (still jiggly in center) "plate" to finish.

The Black Sheep Bistro's
Gateau au Chocolat

1 Cake		2 Cakes
8 oz	Dark Chocolate	16 oz
5	Egg Yolks & Whites separated	10
1/2 cup	Water	1 cup
1/4 cup	Flour	1/2 cup
1/3 cup	Sugar	2/3 cup
1/2 tsp	Vanilla	1 tsp
1/4 lb	Unsalted Butter	1/2 lb

< The secret to this cakes moistness!

Toast fennel seed in pan, add orange, cream and milk. Heat to boiling point. In a bowl mix egg yolks, vanilla and sugar. Strain and add the cream mixture.

Pour into dishes, make water bath and bake.

The Black Sheep Bistro's
Creme de Catalana

1/2 cup Fennel Seeds & 1 Orange (Sliced)
5 cups Heavy Whipping Cream & 1 cup Milk
1tsp Vanilla, 1/2 cup Sugar
12 Eggs Yolks (1+ cup)
Bake at 350° until "done"
(about 45 minutes, depending on size of dish)

Have fun burning the sugar!

Hint - Tilt dish to the side and roll as you burn it!

Profiteroles and Italian Sundaes were very popular!

So simple, so good!

The Black Sheep Bistro's
Italian Sundae

Black Sheep Chocolate Sauce
(see video for Black Sheep Chocolate Sauce)
**Great Vanilla Bean Ice Cream
pour in a Hot Espresso!**

#1 Heat this mix till it pulls away from the pan.

#2 Carefully Adding one egg at a time!

With a pastry bag pipe 2" rounds.

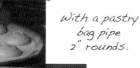

Use a wet finger to tap down points.

The Black Sheep Bistro's
Profiteroles

#1 { melt 1/2 # unsalted butter into 2 cups water
add 1/2 tsp salt & 1 Tbsp sugar
then add 2 cups flour and mix well,
#2 > to finish add 8 eggs, one at a time!
Bake at 350° till golden brown
(about 45 minutes)
This recipe is OK to 1/2 or even 1/4 the amounts!

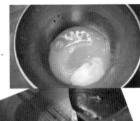

Melt chocolate in water.

Combine eggs & sugar.

Mix together!

Whip cream.

Fold till smooth.
Refrigerate.
Enjoy!

The Black Sheep Bistro's
Chocolate Mousse

1/2		Full
6 (1/2 cup)	eggs yolks	12 (1 cup)
1/2 cup	sugar	1 cup
3 cups	heavy whipping cream	6 cups
8 oz	milk chocolate	1#
8 oz	bittersweet chocolate	1#
1/2 cup	water	1 cup

Fresh Berries

Simply get the best Strawberries, Blueberries, Blackberries and Raspberries and serve them; plain, with whipping cream, with whipped cream, with ice cream, Chocolate Mousse, Chocolate Sauce, or a light sprinkling of sugar!

" Guido" was very popular!

The " Tart's" pastry shell was made in France and was like a vanilla cookie!

The Black Sheep Bistro's
Dressed Up Desserts
Find the best Ice Creams or pre-made favorites and dress them up with chocolate sauces, fruits, fresh mint, hand whipped cream, nuts and more!

(Brother's Desserts in Irvine made our ice creams.)

< Lemon sorbet

We " hand whipped" our cream to order!

The Dark
< Truffle

White Truffle

41

The Black Sheep Bistro's Chef's La Fantasia
Simply the Chef's assortment of three of our favorite desserts!

Break into smaller bits.

Melt, cool, serve!

The Black Sheep Bistro's Chocolate Sauce

Small		Large
1.75 oz	Dark Chocolate	16 oz
1.75 oz	Milk Chocolate	16 oz
1/3 cup	Water	3 3/4 cups

Melt in a pan, cool and serve!

Both these sauces are so quick and easy!

White chocolate

Heavy cream

Melt together

Strain, cool & serve!

White Chocolate Sauce

2 parts White Chocolate Chips
3 parts Heavy Whipping Cream

Blend and melt in a double boiler, strain, cool and serve!

43

Notes

Extras

Sauces & Dressings

Aioli, La Rouille, Tarragon Aioli, and Cliantro Aioli
(The staples that set the tone for much of our cuisine.) - pages 44, 45 & 46

Tomato Provencale - page 47

Harissa Paste - page 47

Honey Lavender Sauce - page 53

House Salad Dressing - page 48

Garlic Butter - page 48

The really important stuff!

Minced Garlic - page 49

Garlic Croutons - page 49

Garlic Mashed Potatoes - page 50

Rice - page 50

Black Sheep Peasant Bread - page 51

Confit of Duck - page 52 & 53
(One of the things we were known best for!)

Starting things off right!
(This is how I started cooking.)

Kids Cold Sauce & Kids Hot Sauce - page 54 & 55

Lambys and Aioli

Probably the most versatile sauces I've ever worked with!

The Black Sheep Bistro's Aioli

In a mixer blend;
1/2 cup finely minced garlic cloves
1 egg yolk* < *Some chefs use more egg for a "heavier" texture.*
Then slowly add 2 cups canola oil,
2 tsp lemon juice & 1 Tbsp red wine vinegar
1/4 + tsp ground white pepper & 1 (+) tsp salt
Then slowly add water to desired consistency
Finish with 1/2 cup extra virgin olive oil < *You can also play with the amount of Olive Oil/Canola Oil if you prefer a heavier Olive Oil taste!*
Aioli should be well seasoned!

It's easy!

Start with Minced Garlic and the egg yolk* (s).

With mixer running; start adding the Canola Oil slowly...

...stop adding oil and let it bind!

Oh yeah! Then there's fish with Aioli & La Rouille!

*We use pasturized egg yolks to help prevent food borne illness.

Our "Grand Aioli" made great use of both Aioli & La Rouille!

Continue adding the oil

Then the lemon, vinegar, salts, pepper...

Room temp water to desired consistency & the final Olive Oil and seasoning!

The Black Sheep Bistro's La Rouille
Follow instructions for
Aioli
Then stir in desired amount of cayenne pepper
La Rouille should be spicy!

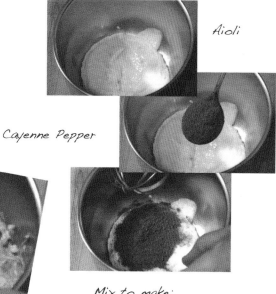

Aioli

Cayenne Pepper

Mix to make;
< La Rouille!

Three Aiolis

Start with the garlic, onions and then with the machine running, the parsley.

The Black Sheep Bistro's
Cilantro Aioli

In a food processor blend; 2 cups each garlic cloves, chopped onion and 1 bunch fresh parsley
Then slowly alternate back and forth;
4 cups canola oil & 1/4 cup red wine vinegar
Add 2 bunches fresh cilantro
1 Tbsp salt & 1 Tbsp Rick's Chef's Salt
3 Tbsp red chili flakes

These are both eggless Aiolis and are made the same way!

Add the oil in a slow stream.

Tarragon Aioli

In a food processor blend; 2 cups each garlic cloves, chopped onion and 1 bunch fresh parsley
Then slowly add 3 cups canola oil
Next add 1 cup Extra Virgin Olive Oil, 4 cups fresh tarragon leaves, 1 + Tbsp salt, 1 1/2 Tbsp Rick's Chef Salt, and 1/4 cup red wine vinegar
Finish with 1 cup canola oil

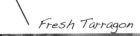

Cilantro & chili flakes   OR   Fresh Tarragon

Remember to taste and taste again!

Add the rest of the ingredients, season and pack for storage or serve!

These sauces should be well seasoned! Some might say strong, but you want a little to go a long way!

48   (To make a Basil Aioli, substitute fresh Basil for the Tarragon.)

The fourth of the Four Seasons sauces!

Here again a simple sauce to make (and it keeps) it's the SEASONING that's so important!

Tomato Olive Provençal

(Thicker or lighter sauce?)

Extra Virgin Olive Oil
Rough Chop Garlic, Diced Onion
Water, Mix of Black & Green Olives,
Basil, Fresh Parsley, Italian Herbs, Thyme
Rick's Chef Salt, Salt
Canned Diced Tomatoes, Tomato Paste (?)

Even Chicken tastes great with Harissa!

This "paste" sould be full of flavor!

Harissa

Put whole peeled Garlic cloves in a food processor, turn it on and add a Paprika you like (I prefer a slightly sweet one), Rick's Chef Salt, Salt, and then spice it up with lots of Cayenne Pepper! Then choose from the following; Caraway Seed, Cumin (just a little), Coriander and any other Middle-Eastern spice you like.
To finish add Extra Virgin Olive Oil and puree to a thick paste. Then add a little Lemon Juice, Rick's Chef Salt, Salt, Paprika and Cayenne Pepper to taste!

The Lamb Chops Harissa were very popular!

49

Do it in the blender. It should be rich and creamy.

Minced garlic and Goat Cheese make this dressing so unique!

The Black Sheep Bistro's
<u>House Salad Dressing</u>

1 spoon each; Basil, Thyme, Italian Herbs
1/2 spoon Ground Black Pepper
2 sp Rick's Chef Salt & 1 1/2 sp Salt
1/2 cup Red Wine Vinegar
2 large spoons Fresh Minced Garlic
2 huge spoons Fresh Goat Cheese
1/2 cup Water (more if needed)
3 3/4 cups Canola Oil

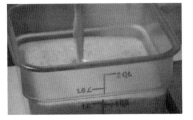

Cut butter into small pieces and drop in one at a time!

<u>Garlic Butter</u>

Blend - 1/2 cup each whole garlic cloves, diced
onion, fresh parsley & 1/4 cup ex. virgin olive oil.
Then add - 1/2 # butter (as shown)
1 (+) tsp Rick's Chef's Salt
1/2 tsp Ground Black Pepper
1/4 tsp Ground White Pepper
This butter should be well seasoned!

Great on steaks, pasta grilled vegetables and more!

Coarse

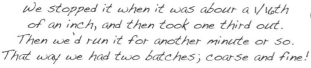

Fine

We stopped it when it was about a 1/16th of an inch, and then took one third out. Then we'd run it for another minute or so. That way we had two batches; coarse and fine!

Minced Garlic

Put whole peeled Garlic cloves in a food processor, turn it on and add Canola Oil and puree to desired texture.

Slice.

Put on;

minced garlic,

Rick's Chef Salt
Herbs de Provence
Paprika...

And toast right before serving!

Salad Croutons
Simply cube leftover French Bread, toss in Rick's Chef Salt and bake on low until crunchy.

Garlic Croutons
Cut leftover French Bread into rounds, smear with Minced Garlic, top with Rick's Chef Salt, Herbs de Provence and Paprika!

We used these for appetizers, Bouillabaisse and more!

51

Season them!

Garlic Mashed Potatoes

**Peel, chop and cook the potatoes.
Transfer to a bowl and whip in Unsalted
Butter, Minced Garlic, Rick's Chef Salt
and Salt to taste!**

We used a pastry bag for decor.

Use a heavy coffee cup as a mold.

Rice
**In a pan heat canola oil
Add; 2 parts Long Grain Rice, heat/set/stir till
lightly browned. Then add; chopped onions,
minced garlic, Rick's Chef Salt and salt.
Stir in 3 parts water.
Bring to a simmer, turn heat to low, lid and
cook 10 minutes. Then turn off heat and set
for 45 minutes. Taste, season and serve.**

*The "trick" to this rice
is to cook it, cover it,
and let it sit undisturbed!*

*Then taste it and season
it again if need be.*

The Black Sheep Bistro's
Peasant Bread

**Combine; 3 1/2 c warm water (110°), 3 c flour,
3 tsp sugar, 1 tsp salt & 3 tsp yeast
- Let sit and rise -
Then add 3 + cups flour to desired consistency
Kneed, shape and bake!**

In the video, before baking, you'll see we rub the top with Rick's Chef Salt, herbs & a small amount of water. You get a better tasting, and firmer crust!

Cassoulet with Confit of Duck was very popular.

Duck Confit

Bone the duck, render the fat, marinate the duck pieces in; garlic, salt, Rick's Chef Salt & herbs for 1 to 6 days. Cook the duck pieces in the rendered duck fat at 200° for 4 hours. Strain the fat and pour over the duck pieces and "age."

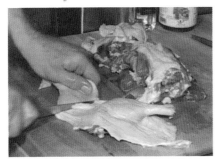

Bone...

Marinate and store till ready to cook.

The fat

Render fat in a pan with water.

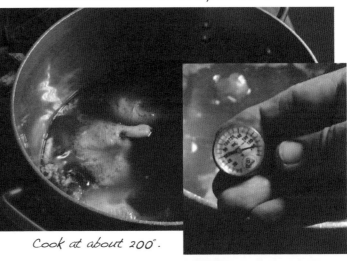

Cook at about 200°.

Remove...

Put in a sealed container and cover with the fat.

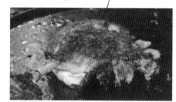

Store in refrigerator till ready.

Strain the rest of the fat and save the thick stock that collects at the bottom.

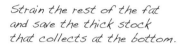

Use this stock with the rest of the ingredients to make the Lavender Sauce.

Rick's Honey Lavender Sauce

Duck Fat, Minced Garlic
3 parts Rich Duck Stock
Lavender Flowers
I part Wildflower Honey
Rick's Chef Salt, Salt

Saute garlic in duck fat, add stock, then lavender flowers, then honey, season (it should be both sweet & salty) with Rick's Chef Salt, salt, bring to a boil, store till needed.

The finished sauce.

Simple set-up; tomato sauce, dried basil and Italian Herbs, Rick's Chef Salt, (or salt & pepper.)

Let them add to their hearts content, but...

Kids "Cold" Pizza Sauce

Put 8 oz of Tomato Sauce (100% tomatoes, no salt!) in a bowl or container;
Let them stir in; Dried Basil, Dried Italian Herbs & either salt and pepper or Rick's Chef Salt to "taste"

...encourage them to; add, then taste, add, then taste...

The finished sauce.

...until it's what tastes good to them!

Have it all out and ready; olive oil, minced garlic, dried basil and Italian Herbs, Rick's Chef Salt, (or just S&P) tomato paste and water.

Kids will find this a great multi-purpose sauce for bread, pasta, vegetables cheese and more!

The "Hot" Pizza Sauce
Saute Chopped Garlic in Extra Virgin Olive Oil
Add; Dried Basil, Dried Italian Herbs
and Rick's Chef Salt
Add some Water, boil then add
Tomato Paste (100% tomatoes, no salt!)
Add more water to desired consistency
Finish by adding Basil, Italian Herbs
& Rick's Chef Salt (or S & P) to "taste".

< My assistant Justin Enayat.

Here again both the learning and the fun comes from the continual addition of ingredients one by one, and the tasting till it's right!
(Note - This is a good exercise for "kids" of all ages. Some may need parental guidence, and some may need their child's guidence.)

57

Also by Rick Boufford, the Black Sheep Bistro's Legacy and more!

   Rick spent almost 5 years shooting his entire menu for the Black Sheep's Video Cookbook. A DVD for both fun and educational purposes. The responses from those who have bought it, used it, and given it as gifts amazed him but also told him there were many who wanted a hard copy for the kitchen. This workbook companion came as a result. For those who missed the DVD, it's available at Amazon.com along with Rick's many other books and DVDs;

Also on DVD!   *Learn about Wine!*

      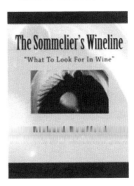

The Black Sheep Bistro's
Video Cookbook Vol 1 - DVD
The entire menu, dish by
dish exactly as it's done
in a professional kitchen.

How To Party Like
A Black Sheep - DVD
Cassoulet, Bouillabaisse,
really big Paella, Le Grand Aioli
and a Kids Pizza Party.

The Sommelier's Wineline
"What To Look For In Wine"
A simple, straight forward
step by step how and why
we do what we do!

Also look for the soon to be released The Black Sheep Bistro's Video Cookbook Vol 2 with all the Specials, soups and vegetables! (Subscribers to the Black Sheep Cooking Club get to preview the videos as there are made!)

Where to go next!

   Through The Black Sheep Cooking Club's web site, Rick shares all he's been privy to enjoy in the culinary arts world now for over 3 decades. Join him, where you'll not only learn to cook and think like a chef, you'll see some of his other favorite things to do; make wood surfboards, make simple jewelry from sea glass, and travel the world shooting wild animals (with a camera of course!) You'll find all of it and more at Just Good Fun.

Join Rick at both these web sites;

blacksheepcookingclub.com & justgoodfun.net

Richard "Rick" Boufford, one of the few Sommelier's in the world, who legally can use the term, "bear breath."

About the Author

Rick's been cooking since he was seven. He's also worked every position of a kitchen, managed the front of the house and became a well respected Sommelier. He and his wife Diana ran their own restaurant, The Black Sheep Bistro (in Tustin, California) for 22 years. Since the sale of the restaurant in January of 2011, Rick says he's still cooking, everyday, and shopping. His new chosen profession is simply to share what he's done over the last 3 decades in the restaurant and hospitality industry, and maybe more importantly, how one can easily apply that in their own home!

Join Rick and learn the way all chefs learn, by watching!
blacksheepcookingclub.com

End Notes

The Black Sheep Bistro's Cookbook Volume 1 - Softcover Book
The companion to;
The Black Sheep Bistro's Video Cookbook Volume 1 - DVD
Both available at Amazon.com
www.justgoodfun.net and www.blacksheepcookingclub.com

Questions or comments please write:
Just Good Fun P.O. Box 15427, Newport Beach, CA 92659-5427